Prophet Stories from the Quran

Including Prophet;

Adam

Nuh

Yusuf

Musa

Written by:

Mohamed Abdelsalam

Illustration Source:

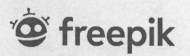 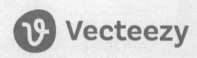

My humble effort I dedicate to my sweet and loving parents
whose affection, love, encouragement and prays make me able
to get such success and honor.

In a very ancient time, Allah was alone and nothing with him.

Allah wanted to create the universe in which we live, so He created the heavens and the earth.

On the earth, Allah created rivers and seas, and the earth grew with grass and trees, and mountains rose on the surface of the earth.

Allah created Adam and his wife Hawwa, and placed Adam and Hawwa in Jannah and told them to eat from the trees of Jannah except for one tree.

Allah warned them against Shaytan, so he told Adam that he is an enemy of you and your wife.

Adam and Hawwa said: Allah, We have made a mistake, and if you do not forgive us and have mercy on us, then we will be among the losers.

Allah accepted the repentance of Adam and Hawwa, forgave them, and sent them down to earth to live on it and to reconstruct the earth. This is how the story of humanity began.

Circle The Right Answer

What was the Lie that Shaytaan told Adam?

If Adam looks at the tree, he will never cry.

If Adam eats from the tree, he will be able to fly.

If Adam eats from the tree, he will never die.

How did Adam feel after he ate from the tree?

Adam felt angry.

Adam felt sorry.

Adam felt happy.

What did Allah then do to Adam?

Allah forgave Adam, but sent him to live on the Earth.

Allah forgave Adam and let him stay in Jannah.

Allah did not forgive Adam and sent him to live on the Earth.

Color The Right answer

Who made the sun, the rivers and the sky?

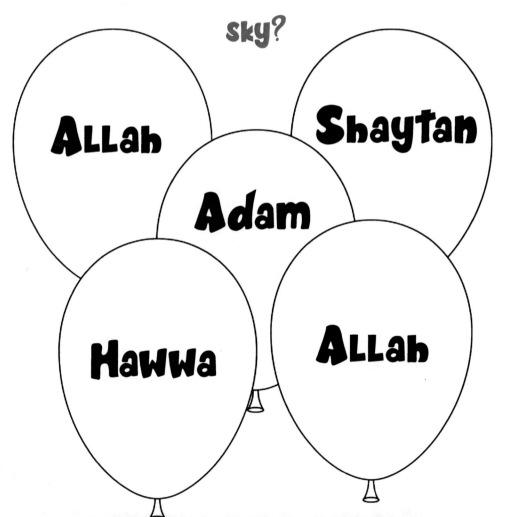

Allah

Shaytan

Adam

Hawwa

Allah

Color The Right answer

Where did Adam first Live?

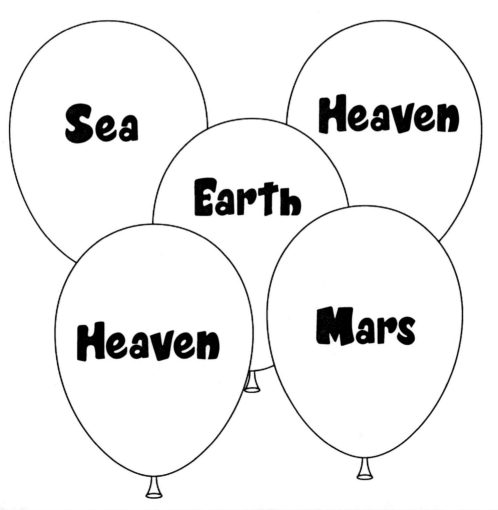

Sea

Heaven

Earth

Heaven

Mars

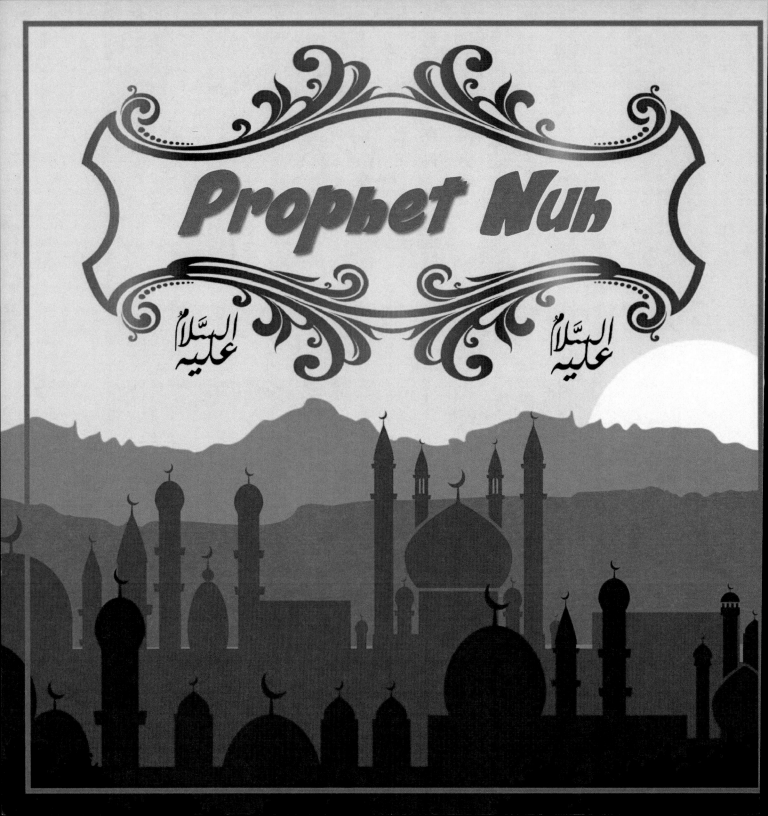

For many generations Nuh's people had been worshipping statues that they called gods. They believed that these gods would bring them good, protect them from evil.

Allah in his mercy sent his messenger Nuh to guide his people. Nuh was an excellent speaker and a very patient man. Nuh's people were divided into two groups after his warning, believer followed him and another mocking.

Nuh chose a place outside the city, far from the sea. HE collected wood and tools and began to day and night to build a ship (The Ark). The people's mockery continued.

After the ship was constructed, Nuh hurried to collect the believers. He also took with him a pair, male and female, of every type of animal, bird and insect.

Allah Commanded water to rose from the cracks in the earth; there was not a crack from which water did not rise. Rain poured from the sky in quantities never seen before on earth.

Water continued pouring from the sky and rising from the cracks; hour after hour the level rose. The seas and waves covered the land.

Nuh called out to his son, who had separated himself (apart), "O my son! Embark with us and be not with the disbelievers." The son replied, "I will climb a mountain, it will save me from the water."

Nuh said: "This day there is no savior from the Decree of Allah except him on whom He has mercy", And a wave came in between them so he (the son) was among the drowned.

The interior of the earth moved in a strange way, and the ocean floors lifted suddenly, flooding the dry land. The earth, for the first time was submerged.

So, the ship sailed with them between high waves like mountains.

With Allah Commands, calm returned to earth, the water level decreased, and the dry land shone once again in the rays of the sun.

Nuh released the birds, and the beats which scattered over the earth. After that the believers disembarked.

Following the disembarkation there was a day of fasting in thanks to Allah.

Nuh and the believers started planting the earth again.

Write in your own words what you have Learned from this story?

1

2

3

Match the right answer

Yusuf was born and grew up in land of Canaan (Palestine), He was respectful, kind and considerate. His brother Benjamin was equally pleasant. Both were from one mother.

One evening Yusuf saw a dream. When he woke up, he went to his father (Jacob) and said to him, "Father, I have seen eleven planets, the sun and the moon prostrating to me."

Yusuf's brothers felt angry and decided to get rid of him. The brothers asked their father to let Yusuf go with them to play, and Jacob agreed.

On leaving home, they went directly to the well, they threw Yusuf in it, after they removed his shirt and painting it with sheep's blood.

In the evening, they returned to their father crying and said: "O our father We went racing with one another and left Yusuf by our belongings, and the wolf ate him, this is his shirt."

Their father (Jacob) knew that his beloved son was still alive and that his other sons were lying. The father acted wisely by praying for mighty patience.

A caravan on its way to Egypt passed by the well. A man lowered in his bucket for water. The man shocked when he found a young boy in the well.

The man shouted to his friends who helped him to pull out Yusuf. Then Caravan took Yusuf along to Egypt, far away from his beloved homeland to sell him.

All over the Egyptian city the news spread that an unusually handsome, Strong young boy was on sale. The Chief Minister of Egypt (the Aziz) saw Yusef in the market , he liked him and bought him.

The Aziz took Yusuf to his house, and his wife was happy with the boy, because she did not have children. The Aziz said to her: "We will adopt him as a son"

Yusuf's grew up and his handsomeness became the talk of the town. People referred to him as the most attractive man they had ever seen. The chief minister's wife, could not resist the handsome Yusuf, and She fell in love with him.

one day she offered Yusuf her love, but he refused and moved to the door to escape, she ran after him, and her husband saw them at the door. She accused Yusuf and her husband decided to put Yusuf in prison.

When the two men asked Yusuf about the dreams, he said that the cook would be crucified until he died, while the cupbearer would return to the service of the king. Yusuf asked the cupbearer to tell the king about him, but he forgot.

When the news reached the cupbearer, he remembered Yusuf. The cupbearer ran to the king to tell him about Yusuf, who was the only one capable to interpreting the dream. The king sent the cupbearer to ask him about it.

Yusuf interpreted it to him: "There will be seven years of abundance. There will be an excess of good harvest, more than the people will need. This should be stored. Thereafter, seven years of famine will follow, during which time the excess grain could be used."

He also advised that during the famine they should save some grain to be used for seed for the next harvest. The cupbearer hurried back with the good news. The king was happy with Yusuf's interpretation.

The king commanded that Yusuf be set free from prison and offered him a high position as minister to had full control over the cultivation, and crops storage.

Yusuf ordered of wheat and grain cultivation during the good seven years, and storage of crops in warehouses to protect the country in the seven years of famine.

Indeed, the years of abundance have passed and the years of famine have come. The famine spread throughout the region, including Canaan, the homeland of Yusuf.

Jacob sent ten of his sons, all except one (Benjamin), to Egypt to buy grain. When Yusuf saw them, he immediately recognized his brothers, but they did not know him. To them Yusuf no longer existed, he is dead.

Yusuf asked them to bring their younger brother (Benjamin) to give them grain. The brothers returned to their father Jacob and asked him to send Benjamin with them. Jacob agreed, after they swore to protect him.

As soon as Yusuf saw his little brother, he took him to a far place and said to him: "I am your brother Yusuf, do not mention that to your brothers"

Yusuf asked the servants to supply his brothers with grains and to put the king's gold cup in his brother's bag. As soon as Yusuf's brothers moved, the soldiers shouted at them "O you travelers, you are thieves!"

brothers inquired: "What have you lost?". The soldiers said "you stole the king's golden cup". When Yusuf searched them, he found the king's golden cup in his brother's bag.

Yusuf's brothers returned to their father and told him what had happened. Jacob grieved for his son and remembered Yusuf, so he continued to cry until he lost his sight. Yusuf's brothers returned to Egypt again, begging Yusuf to release their brother.

Yusuf said to them: "Did you know what you did to Yusuf and his brother". At this moment they recognized him. Yusuf said: "Do not be afraid, I will not punish you".

Yusuf gave them his shirt and asked them to return to their father, and to throw his shirt on their father's face so that he could see again, and he asked them to come to live in Egypt. Indeed, the brothers returned to Jacob and when they put the shirt on his face, he returned with sight.

Jacob and his family went to Egypt and entered unto Yusuf while he was sitting on the throne, and they fell down before him prostrate. This was interpretation of his dream

Write in your own words what you have Learned from this story?

1 _____
_____
_____
_____

2 _____
_____
_____
_____

3 _____
_____
_____
_____

Color The Right answer

The Caravan took Joseph along to

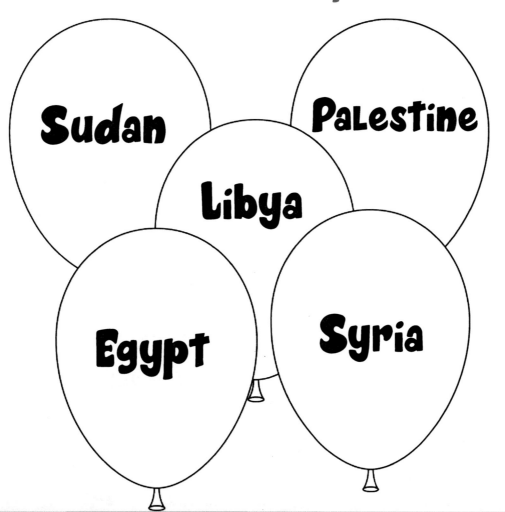

Sudan

Palestine

Libya

Egypt

Syria

A mighty Pharaoh ruled Egypt, whom the Egyptians worshiped, and this Pharaoh saw the Children of Israel multiplying and prospering. Therefore, he oppressed them.

So, he took their lands and possessions and then tortured them severely. He used to take their women to serve and use the men in the most severe work for small wages or nothing

One day, Pharaoh had a dream that a baby boy would be born into the children of Israel would one day kill Pharaoh. Therefore, so Pharaoh commanded to kill every baby boys born to the children of Israel.

At this time Musa was born . Then Allah commanded his mother to make a small box for Moses and put him into the box, and throw him into the river.

Musa's mother sent her daughter to follow the box. Eventually, the basket washed up from the River Nile right near Pharaoh's palace.

At this time, Pharaoh's wife went out near the Nile, who was a good woman, and she saw the box and Musa. She loved him, and decided to adopt him as a son.

The queen asked for a few nurses to nurse Moses, but he refused. The queen was distressed and sent for more nurses. Musa's sister said that she knew jut the nurse who would nurse the baby, so Musa returned to his mother.

Musa grew up in the pharaoh palace. Allah had granted Musa good health, strength, knowledge, and wisdom. So, The weak turned to him for protection and justice.

One day, Musa saw two men fighting. One was an Israelite, who was being beaten by the other, an Egyptian. the Israelite begged Musa for help.

Musa intervened and removed the oppressor with his hand and killed him by mistake. Musa's heart was filled with sorrow, and begged Allah for forgiveness.

Musa begged Allah to forgive him, but he was afraid of Pharaoh revenge, so he left Egypt in a hurry. Musa walked until he reached a city called Madyan.

Musa noticed a group of shepherds watering their animals, and he found two women preventing their sheep from mixing with the flocks of the others.

So he went and asked them about the reason for shepherding the sheep by themselves. The younger sister said: "Our father is an old man; his health is too poor for him to go outdoors for shepherding."

so he watered the sheep for them, with the rest of the shepherds.

The two girls told their father about Musa and asked him to thank Musa. Musa went to meet their father who offered him to stay with them and marry to one of his daughters on condition that he agree to work for a period of eight years.

Musa agreed and lived with them for ten years, then he decided to return to Egypt. On the way, Musa saw a burning fire, and when he came to it, Allah called him and told him that he is the Messenger of Allah to pharaoh and his people to warn them tell them about Allah .

Musa asked God to send his brother Haroon with him to Pharaoh. Musa and Haroon went together to pharaoh asking him to worship the one God (Allah). Pharaoh mocked them and said: "I will imprison you."

Musa said: I brought you the evidence! So Musa threw his stick, and it turned into a big snake, and he drew out his hand, and it was white as snow.

Pharaoh thought that Musa and Haroon are two magicians, so he challenged that he would bring the cleverest magicians in the country to beat them, and they agreed.

On the festival day, Musa and the magicians came, the magicians threw their magical objects down on the ground and it took the forms of snakes. Then Musa threw his stick it became a big snake which ate all the magicians' snakes.

When the magicians saw the power of Musa, they Said: "We believe in the God of Musa and Haroon.". The crowd rose like a great wave, and screaming with excitement. Pharaoh threatened the magicians to cut off their hands and feet and to tie them on the trunks of palm trees.

Allah commanded Musa to take the children of Israel and leave. When they reached the sea shore, they found Pharaoh in their tracks to attack them. Allah commanded Musa to Smite the sea with his stick, the sea parted and they crossed.

After they crossed, Pharaoh and his soldiers tried to follow Musa and the children of Israel, the waters closed over him, drowning him and his entire army.

Musa and the children of Israel entered Sinai, and there Allah commanded Musa to ascend the Mount al-Tour. Over the mountain, Musa was given the Torah that show good and evil to the children of Israel as a light for guidance.

Write a summary of the story in 3 sentences

1 _____
_____
_____
_____
_____

2 _____
_____
_____
_____
_____

3 _____
_____
_____
_____
_____

Match the right answer

Made in United States
North Haven, CT
26 April 2022

18605414R00031